CITY OF AMBITION

AMBITION

ARTISTS &

NEW YORK

1900–1960

Elisabeth Sussman WITH **John G. Hanhardt**
AND ASSISTED BY **Corey Keller**

WITH AN ESSAY BY **Brendan Gill**

Whitney Museum of American Art NEW YORK
IN ASSOCIATION WITH
Flammarion Paris–New York

CITY OF
MBITION

23

25

24

This book was published on the occasion of
the exhibition "NYNY: City of Ambition" at the Whitney Museum of American Art,
July 3–October 27, 1996.

The exhibition is sponsored by **DKNY**

Additional support has been provided by
Laurie Tisch Sussman *and*
The Horace W. Goldsmith Foundation.

Research for the exhibition and publication was supported by
income from an endowment established by Henry and Elaine Kaufman,
The Lauder Foundation, Mrs. William A. Marsteller, The Andrew W. Mellon
Foundation, Mrs. Donald A. Petrie, Primerica Foundation,
Samuel and May Rudin Foundation, Inc., The Simon Foundation,
and Nancy Brown Wellin.

This publication was organized at
the Whitney Museum by Mary
E. DelMonico, Head, Publications;
Sheila Schwartz, Editor;
Heidi Jacobs, Copy Editor; Nerissa
Dominguez, Production
Coordinator; José Fernández,
Assistant/Design; Melinda Barlow,
Assistant; and Elizabeth Edge,
Intern.

Design: Barbara Glauber
Design Assistance: Beverly Joel
Printing: Meridian Printing
Binding: Acme Bookbinding
Printed and bound in the USA

Published by the Whitney Museum
of American Art
945 Madison Avenue, New York,
New York 10021

ISBN 0-87427-108-8 paper (WMAA)
ISBN 2-08013-628-3 cloth
(Flammarion)

Flammarion
26 rue Racine
75006 Paris
Numéro d'édition: 1199
Dépôt légal: July 1996

FULL DATA FOR CAPTIONS
TO REPRODUCED WORKS CAN BE
FOUND IN THE WORKS IN THE
EXHIBITION, BEGINNING ON P. 134.

Cover image: Thurman Rotan,
Skyscrapers, 1932

Library of Congress Cataloging-
in-Publication Data
City of ambition: artists and New
York, 1900–1960 / organized
by Elisabeth Sussman.; film program
by John G. Hanhardt; with
an introduction by Brendan Gill.
  p.   cm.
"An exhibition of paintings, sculp-
ture, films, and prints that capture
how New York has inspired an
unprecedented artistic outpouring
from 1900–1960"—T.p. verso.
ISBN 0-87427-108-8 (alk. paper)
1. New York (N.Y.) in art—
Exhibitions 2. Arts, American—
New York (State)—New York
(N.Y.)—Exhibitions. 3. Arts,
Modern—20th century—New York
(State)—New York (N.Y.)—
Exhibitions.
I. Sussman, Elisabeth, 1939-   .
II. Hanhardt, John G. III. Whitney
Museum of American Art.
NX511.N4N96 1996
700'.97471 0747471—dc20
    96-20431
    CIP

"The Heart of Harlem," from
Collected Poems by Langston
Hughes. ©1994 by the Estate of
Langston Hughes. Reprinted
by permission of Alfred A. Knopf Inc.

Excerpt from *The Group* ©1963
Mary McCarthy, renewed 1991
by James Raymond West. Reprinted
by permission of Harcourt Brace
& Company and Mary McCarthy
Literary Trust.

"English Sparrows (Washington
Square)" by Edna St. Vincent
Millay. From COLLECTED POEMS,
HarperCollins. ©1939, 1967
by Edna St. Vincent Millay and
Norma Millay Ellis. All rights
reserved. Reprinted by permission
of Elizabeth Barnett, literary
executor.

TAKE ME BACK TO MANHATTAN,
by Cole Porter, ©1930 (Renewed)
Warner Bros. Inc. All Rights
Reserved. Used by Permission.
WARNER BROS. PUBLICATIONS U.S.
INC., Miami, FL 33014

"The Lure of New York," from
E.B. WHITE: WRITINGS FROM THE
NEW YORKER, 1925–1976
(HarperCollins). ©1937, 1965 E.B.
White. Originally in *The*
New Yorker. All rights reserved.

CONTENTS

EDWARD HOPPER, **Early Sunday Morning**, 1930

WHITNEY MUSEUM
OF AMERICAN ART
OFFICERS AND TRUSTEES

DIRECTOR'S FOREWORD

T hough it may sound obvious, the Whitney Museum is indeed fortunate to have been founded and located in New York City. For one doubts that an institution dedicated to the once unheard-of and still often controversial concept of celebrating American art in its time could have flourished in any other metropolis. But in fact it was not mere fate that inspired Gertrude Vanderbilt Whitney's decision to buck tradition and devote herself to the creation of this museum of American art. It was the same force that drove her and the artists of her time to forge new ways of expressing the energy and spirit of the essential twentieth-century city. It was the x-factor that provoked the imagining of a city of skyscraping buildings. It was the primal force that in many ways defines New York. Simply stated, it was pure, unfettered ambition.

As curator Elisabeth Sussman notes in her introduction to this provocative and delight-filled exhibition, "NYNY: City of Ambition" takes its title from the 1910 Alfred Stieglitz photograph of the then-burgeoning New York skyline. But the purpose of this exhibition is to explore the notion of ambition itself. Focusing attention on the flourishing creative ferment of the first half of the century, the exhibition attempts to locate, reveal, and revel

CHARLES JAMES,
Evening Bolero,
1954

in ambition as an idealized source of energy and inspiration. Exploring painting, printmaking, sculpture, photography, film, fashion, and architecture, the exhibition accords a broad overview of the visual arts, and supports the idea that the real heart of this or any city—and its truest measure—is the art that it has produced.

We are quite proud to present this exhibition, constructed in large part from the Permanent Collection of the Whitney Museum and graced with loans from private and public collections. We thank the lenders for their generosity and their willingness to share their treasures with our audience. I would also like to acknowledge and thank curator Elisabeth Sussman, who undertook this exhibition with intelligence, flair, and good humor. Equally deserving of recognition is the Museum's curator of film and video, John G. Hanhardt, who worked closely with Sussman to integrate a series of significant independent films directly into the exhibition. Corey Keller and Cassi Albinson oversaw the manifold details of the exhibition and catalogue with exceptional dedication and sensitive judgment.

We are pleased and honored by the presence in this volume of the great writer Brendan Gill, friend and former Trustee of the Museum and a legendary New Yorker. Few can express as clearly as he a love and deep respect for this city and its varied and various ambitions.

Collaborating with the curators on the design and physical conceptualization of the exhibition has been the extraordinarily creative designer and problem-solver Tibor Kalman. The Museum is deeply grateful for the time, energy, and wonderful imagination he has devoted to this project. Dan Okrent has selected a glorious group of literary texts to accompany the images in the show. Working under extreme deadline pressures, the Museum's head of publications, Mary DelMonico, and the entire staff of the publications department deserve special recognition for service above and beyond.

Finally, on behalf of the Museum I would like to thank the funders of this exhibition, beginning with our sponsor, Donna Karan New York. We are also grateful for the support of Laurie Tisch Sussman and our friends at the Horace W. Goldsmith Foundation. Without their enlightened generosity, ambitious exhibitions like this would not be possible.

DAVID A. ROSS
Alice Pratt Brown Director

PREFACE

In the nineteenth century, America was renowned for her wide open spaces, majestic mountains, and clear lakes. To natives and foreigners alike, the image of this country was inscribed by a sense of vastness and of the natural wonders of the land. By the early twentieth century, however, the wonder of America lay in its metropolises, and New York—with its towering skyscrapers, bustling streets, flashing signs, and dense commercial districts—was the jewel in the crown.

By 1910, the lower end of the island was filling up with tall buildings. Alfred Stieglitz directed his camera at some of the steeples of commerce and called the photograph *The City of Ambition*. That image said it all—the splendor of the skyscraper had superseded nature. The skyscraper was a miracle of human ingenuity, and the higher it went, the more clever appeared its maker. In a view taken from across the river, *The City of Ambition* pictured a skyline of smoke-spurting minarets, a city of power, wealth, and luxury. Fast forward to the 1940s, to Will Eisner's comic strip, *The Spirit*. The hero lives in a graveyard, beyond the city's limits, and he returns from that netherworld to fight crime in the urban streets. Between Eisner and Stieglitz—between the sparkling wonder of the skyline and the teeming pavements or seedy run-down hangouts on forgotten streets—lies a remarkable variety of images of this amazing city.

Artists of all kinds have flocked to New York, and it is they who have plucked from the city's visual cacophony those singular images that collectively describe urban life. Like the city, the artists in this book are diverse—traditional and avant-garde, independent artists who show in galleries and museums and commercial artists who work for newspapers, magazines, and the fashion industry. To respect that diversity yet provide an underlying narrative, the order imposed on the images in this book is chronological. Beginning with iconic photographs of New York taken in the first decade of the century, we move on to the modernism of the teens and twenties, when sleek outlines and geometric forms shaped urban views. Following is a section on the skyscraper, heralded as one of the enduring images of New York, and here celebrated by photographers, fashion designers, painters. In the 1930s, during the Depression, the attention of artists turned to the people of this city, to workers in their habitual rhythms. New York seemed to come of age during World War II: while much of Europe was going up in flames, the neon lights of Broadway burned bright and nightclubs and street life flourished. After the war, the international character of New York made it the home of the new United Nations and the glamour of the City of Ambition resurfaced in immense new urban projects and a revolutionary cultural renaissance.

ALFRED STIEGLITZ, **The City of Ambition**, 1910

Every image of New York is but one take on the city. Collectively, the works in this book speak not only of the diverse responses the city generates, but as well of New York's provocative allure for artists, who return again and again, decade after decade, to its creative wellspring.

ELISABETH SUSSMAN

11

ALVIN LANGDON COBURN, **Ferryboat, New York Harbor**, 1910

ALVIN LANGDON COBURN, **Brooklyn Bridge, New York**, 1911

EDWARD HOPPER, **Queensborough Bridge**, 1913

GEORGIA O'KEEFFE, **East River from the Shelton**, 1927–28

GEORGE C. AULT, **From Brooklyn Heights**, 1925

GEORGIA O'KEEFFE, **East River, No. 3**, 1926

STEPHAN HIRSCH, **New York, Lower Manhattan**, 1921

JOHN MARIN, **Region of Brooklyn Bridge Fantasy**, 1932

ELSIE DRIGGS, **Queensborough Bridge**, 1927

MINNA WRIGHT CITRON, **Staten Island Ferry**, 1937

21

JOSEPH STELLA, Sketch for **Brooklyn Bridge**, n.d.

JOSEPH STELLA, **The Brooklyn Bridge: Variation on an Old Theme**, 1939

BRENDAN GILL

LONGED-FOR NEIGHBORS

The art historian E.H. Gombrich said long ago that there is no such thing as art; there are only artists. Academics like to play amusing semantic tricks of this sort, thumbing their noses at logic—if there is no such thing as art, then he and his colleagues are claiming to be historians of a subject that doesn't exist. No matter! It is true in principle that any discussion of art should address itself more closely to the thing made than to the maker of the thing. All the more agreeable, then, to find the great Gombrich seeming to endorse a temptation that our contemporary Western culture is irresistibly drawn to—that of placing an emphasis on individuals as marketable commodities every bit as precious as the products of their hands and eyes. How greedy we are to learn the last scrap of personal information about artists! And, alas, in most cases the more scandalous the scrap the more we relish it. Shamelessly, we shiver with pleasure at the mention of Van Gogh's ear. In our day, is so-and-so a falling-down drunk as well as a superb artist? Then let us save talk of her paintings for another day. Does so-and-so favor pretty boys over pretty girls? Plenty of time to discuss his marvelous talent on a more convenient occasion.

Fortunately, there are levels of information-seeking higher than that of tabloid gossip. It has always been a legitimate activity of scholars (this was, of course, the point of Gombrich's remark) to "locate" the artist in respect to the time, place, and circumstances in which he flourished or failed to flourish. For all that most of us know to the contrary, even Van Gogh's nicked-off ear may be found to have some genuine connection with a certain yellow chair and the manner in which he painted it, just as Monet's green thumb led him straight to all those damnable acres of water lilies.

In something like the same fashion, scholars (and we who are not scholars but only scholars-manqués, defined by Muriel Spark as "scholar-monkeys") are justified in seeking out the physical environment of artists, as a means of providing us with clues to their intentions. We are said to be what we eat—a possible defense of cannibalism—but we are also where and how we choose to live. This is especially true of artists who, as in the present exhibition, appear to possess a close relationship to their subject matter. They are artists intensely urban, intensely in and of New York. It would be sentimental—and not necessarily accurate—to call them lovers of New York simply because they have made it a favorite subject; there must have been times, after all, when Canaletto wished

MAURICE PRENDERGAST,
Sailboat Pond, Central Park, c. 1902

Venice would pitch headlong into the sea. Still, the fact is that they went on working here, those New Yorkers of the period between 1900 and 1960, in spite of difficulties that one might have expected to send them bolting elsewhere.

From its beginnings as a trading post in the seventeenth century, New York has indeed been a "City of Ambition," but its ambition has been almost entirely commercial. To the Dutch, money-grubbing was foremost among the virtues, and the polyglot land speculators who succeeded them were content to pursue the same bent. (On his deathbed, John Jacob Astor offered no pious ejaculations. To the family hovering over him, he whispered that his only regret was that he had failed to purchase *all* of Manhattan island.) Most of the nabobs of the nineteenth century, when they thought of art at all, thought of it as the currency of a social realm that their wives were striving to enter; the paintings they accumulated were not merely fashionable interior decoration, purchasable by the yard, but the means of their transformation from outsiders to insiders. Artists were either gifted simpletons or rogues, and the less one saw of them in the big houses lumbering up Fifth Avenue (Henry James was the first to call them white elephants), the better for everyone concerned.

By the early years of the twentieth century, matters had somewhat improved in the world of the arts. Some of the nabobs of the second and third generation were going so far as to buy works of art because they liked them. Others took advice from dealers who had added knowledge to their native cunning—if here on your grand doorstep stood ebullient salesman Joe Duveen, lemur-like on his shoulder perched the suave authenticator Berenson. Moreover, a handful of collectors had been born with that indispensable attribute, flair, commonly defined as intuitive discernment—one thinks of the Havemeyers and especially of Gertrude Vanderbilt Whitney, who made art as well as bought it and by her generosity to fellow artists proceeded to transform a studio on Eighth Street into the quasi-public Whitney Studio and then into a great museum of American art.

Appropriately enough, the geography of the art to which this exhibition is devoted can be imagined as having

JOHN SLOAN, **Backyards, Greenwich Village**, 1914

its center just there on Gertrude Whitney's Eighth Street. (By a coincidence of no great importance, it was in what had been the stable of an immense white marble house adjacent to Whitney's studio that the Metropolitan Museum may be said to have been born.) Thrusting out from this bull's-eye in ever-expanding circles, our imaginary geography includes Washington Square, Greenwich Village—as different from Washington Square as chalk from cheese—Little Italy, the Lower East Side, the Bowery, Chelsea, Times Square, and Central Park. The farthest reach of this Manhattan extends from the harbor to Harlem and amounts to a sizable portion of what is, after all, but a tiny island, held (again to quote Henry James) "in the easy embrace of its great, good-natured rivers, very much as a battered and accommodating beauty may sometimes be 'distinguished' by a gallant less fastidious, with his open arms, than his type would seem to imply." How the members of the Ashcan School would have rejoiced to encounter such a bawdy tribute to their city, especially from such an unlikely source, but the odds are high that they never troubled to read James, as James—friend of Sargent and LaFarge—would surely never have troubled to seek out their work. "Ashcan?" he would have asked. "What on earth is an ashcan? May one dare to speculate on the possibility that it is the approximate equivalent of a dustbin?"

Fascinating for us, at this late date, to speculate on the actual habitations of the sixty-odd artists and photographers making up the present exhibition. Coveys of scholars are no doubt in possession of the facts, accurate down to the number of the street on which the artist lived and the years, months, and days of his residing there, but those of us who are only scholar-monkeys must fall back upon the chance-taking of intuition, all too often the twin brother of invention. I know where I wish these artists to have lived, and my wish will place them there willy-nilly—Ernest Lawson on the banks of the Hudson, Joseph Stella in Brooklyn Heights, Edward Steichen in midtown. It is a necessary accompaniment to the delight I take in John Sloan for him to have lived in the midst of the scenes he painted—somewhere in the Village, say, in a red-brick house not in the best of repair, from a rear window of which one looked out to see a raggedy cat howling and arching its back on a neighboring garden fence. As for Maurice Prendergast, with a seeming perversity I prefer to think of him as *not* living near Central Park, which he so often depicted, but as coming to it from a distance and hugging it to him as the reward for a quest successfully accomplished: the park as an earthly paradise at journey's end.

By the beginning of the twentieth century, the city of ambition had acquired the knack of sheltering artists. The sidewalks I walk on, the doorways I enter, the rooftrees I sleep beneath, however unreliably I may seek to identify them with the artists that have preceded me, are settings in which I sense their ghostly invisible presences. They give me two New Yorks to be nourished by, theirs and mine, and not for the world would I surrender either. Here, harsh and douce, is the city they and we have chosen. How lucky we are to share it with them!

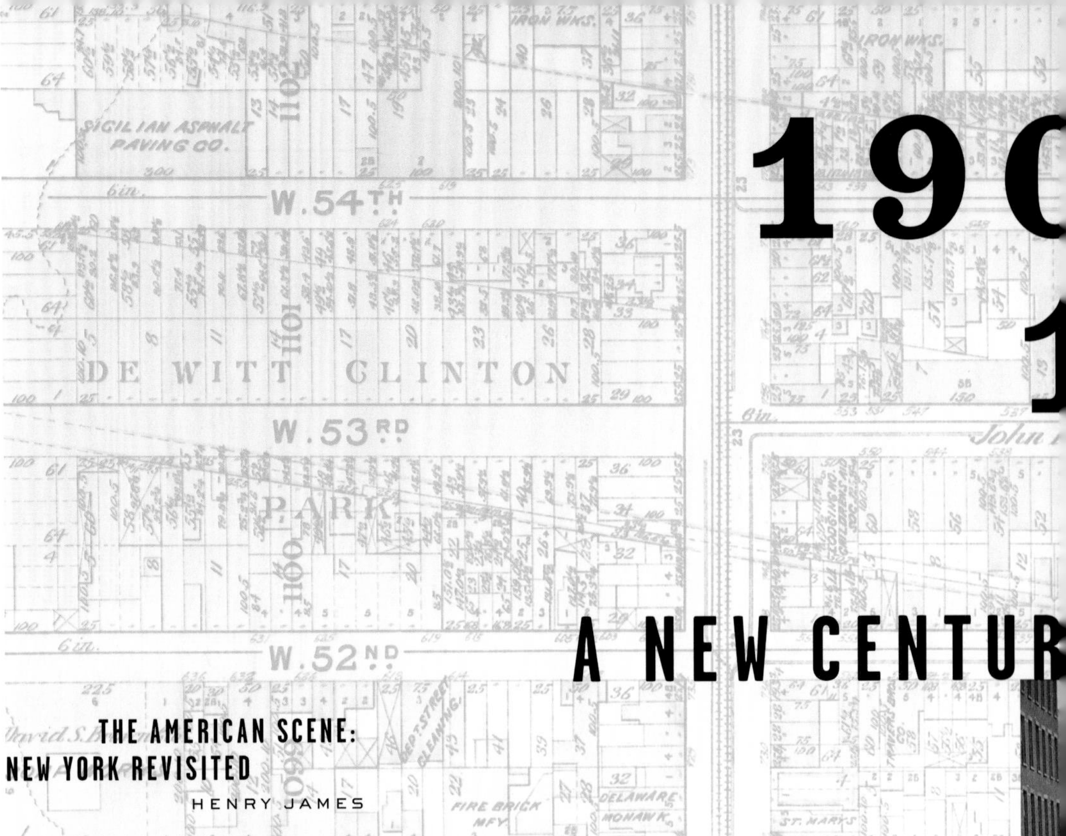

190

1

A NEW CENTUR

THE AMERICAN SCENE: NEW YORK REVISITED

HENRY JAMES

Therefore it is that I find myself rather backward
with a perceived sanction, of an at all proportionate
kind, for the fine exhilaration with which, in this
free wayfaring relation to them, the wide waters of New
York inspire me. There is the beauty of light and air,
the great scale of space, and, seen far away to the west,
the open gates of the Hudson, majestic in their degree,
even at a distance, and announcing still nobler things.
But the real appeal, unmistakably, is in that note
of vehemence in the local life of which I have spoken, for
it is the appeal of a particular type of dauntless power.

The aspect the power wears then is indescrib-
able; it is the power of the most extravagant of cities,
rejoicing, as with the voice of the morning, in its might,
its fortune, its unsurpassable conditions, and impart-
ing to every object and element, to the motion and
expression of every floating, hurrying, panting thing,
to the throb of ferries and tugs, to the plash of waves
and the play of winds and the glint of lights and
the shrill of whistles and the quality and authority of
breeze-borne cries—all, practically, a diffused,
wasted clamour of *detonations*—something of its sharp
free accent and, above all, of its sovereign sense of
being "backed" and able to back.

AMERICA CAME OF AGE at the beginning of the twentieth century, and nowhere was this more evident than in New York City. It was a time of unprecedented expansion: tall buildings, great bridges, and an extensive subway system were under construction. By 1900, the Port of New York had become the busiest in the world. Its majestic ships and graceful bridges soon came to fascinate artists, from photographer Karl Struss to painter Edward Hopper.

The construction of the Flatiron Building (1902) marked the dawn of the skyscraper era. It was the tallest building north of the financial district, and its distinctive triangular profile—like the prow of a great ship—became a symbol of New York's progress. Only eleven years later, the Woolworth Building was completed; sixty stories high, it was the world's tallest building until the completion of the Chrysler Building in 1930. At its dedication, the Woolworth Building was aptly described as a "cathedral of commerce."

For photographers, among them Alfred Stieglitz, Paul Strand, and Alvin Langdon Coburn, the skyscraper was an endless source of wonder and inspiration.

During these years, photography developed as a expressive visual medium, perfectly suited to documenting and depicting the modernization of New York City. Artists such as J. Alden Weir and Ernest Lawson, working in more traditional media, found another kind of poetry in the metropolis, in the city's twilights and clouds of industrial steam.

The first two decades of the twentieth century also saw the arrival of wave upon wave of immigrants: from 1880 to 1919, 17 million immigrants came to the United States through New York City. Many of them settled here, finding work in the city's garment industry and factories. As the population of ethnic neighborhoods like Little Italy and the Lower East Side swelled and overflowed, photographers Alice Austen and Lewis W. Hine and painter George Luks captured the press and bustle of overcrowded tenements and chaotic streets.

UNKNOWN PHOTOGRAPHER, **Partially Clad Skeleton of the Flatiron Building, As Seen from Madison Square**, 1902

ALVIN LANGDON COBURN, **The Octopus**, 1912

PAUL STRAND, **Wall Street, New York**, 1915

KARL STRUSS, **Pennsylvania Station, New York**, 1911

JOHN SLOAN, **Night Windows**, 1910

JOHN SLOAN, **Roofs, Summer Night**, 1906

KARL STRUSS, **Brooklyn Bridge from Ferry Slip, Late Afternoon**, 1913

KARL STRUSS, **Construction—"Excuse Me"**, 1911

WILLIAM J. GLACKENS, **Hammerstein's Roof Garden**, C. 1901

ERNEST LAWSON, **High Bridge—Early Moon**, c. 1910

ALICE AUSTEN, **Ragpickers and Handcarts, 23rd Street and Third Ave., N.Y.**, c. 1896

J. ALDEN WEIR, **The Bridge: Nocturne (Nocturne: Queensboro Bridge)**, c. 1910

J. ALDEN WEIR, **The Plaza: Nocturne**, 1911

43

GEORGE BELLOWS, **Pennsylvania Station Excavation**, 1909

45

ENGLISH SPARROWS
(WASHINGTON SQUARE)

EDNA ST. VINCENT MILLAY

How sweet the sound in the city an hour before sunrise,
When the park is empty and grey and the light clear and
    so lovely
I must sit on the floor before my open window for an hour
    with my arms on the sill
And my cheek on my arm, watching the spring sky's
Soft suffusion from the roofed horizon upward with palest
    rose,
Doting on the charming sight with eyes
Open, eyes closed;
Breathing with quiet pleasure the cool air cleansed by
    the night, lacking all will
To let such happiness go, nor thinking the least thing ill
In me for such indulgence, pleased with the day and with
    myself. How sweet
The noisy chirping of the urchin sparrows from crevice and
    shelf
Under my window, and from down there in the street,
Announcing the advance of the roaring competitive day with
    city bird-song.

A bumbling bus
Goes under the arch. A man bareheaded and alone
Walks to a bench and sits down.
He breathes the morning with me; his thoughts are his own.
Together we watch the first magnanimous
Rays of the sun on the tops of greening trees and on houses
    of red brick and of stone.

1915 – 1925

THE MODERN CITY

THE MODERN CITY, with its tall buildings, crowded streets, and glittering lights, inspired an appropriately innovative artistic response in the teens and early twenties. During this period, artists translated the architecture and the energy of the metropolis into abstract and prismatic city views. Influenced by such European art movements as Cubism and Futurism, John Marin, Max Weber, and Abraham Walkowitz were among the modernist painters who sought to capture the sensation, the pulse—the *experience*—of New York City. Some artists responded to the city with Dada humor: Man Ray's sculpture *New York 17* uses a leaning "tower" and a carpenter's vise to playfully convey the feeling of congested midtown Manhattan.

For some New Yorkers, the twenties were years of high living. The glamour and excess of the era provoked such artistic responses as F. Scott Fitzgerald's chronicle of the Jazz Age, *The Great Gatsby* (1925), and Florine Stettheimer's painting *Spring Sale at Bendel's* (1921). In the 1920s, fashion magazines such as *Vogue* flourished, while artist Edward Steichen and others elevated fashion photography and celebrity portraiture to an art form.

MAX WEBER, **New York Department Store (An Idea of A Modern Department Store)**, 1915

JOHN MARIN, **Lower Manhattan
(Composing Derived from Top of Woolworth)**, 1922

CHARLES SHEELER,
New York, Towards the
Woolworth Building, 1920

ABRAHAM WALKOWITZ, **Cityscape**, c. 1915

MAN RAY, **New York 17**, 1917

FLORINE STETTHEIMER, **Spring Sale at Bendel's**, 1921

EDWARD STEICHEN, **Vionnet Model Imported by Saks-Fifth Avenue**, 1923

JAN MATULKA, **New York Evening**, 1925

EDWARD HOPPER, **Night in the Park**, 1921

EDWARD HOPPER, **Night Shadows**, 1921

TAKE ME BACK TO MANHATTAN

COLE PORTER

The more I travel across the gravel,
The more I sail the sea,
The more I feel convinced of the fact
New York's the town for me.
Its crazy skyline is right in my line,
And when I'm far away
I'm able to bear it for several hours,
And then break down and say:

Take me back to Manhattan,
Take me back to New York,
I'm just longing to see once more
My little home on the hundredth floor.
Can you wonder I'm gloomy?
Can you smile when I frown?
I miss the East Side, the West Side,
The North Side and the South Side,
So take me back to Manhattan,
That dear old dirty town.

1925 – 1932

REACHING FOR THE SKY

MIDTOWN MANHATTAN EXPLODED in the twenties and thirties. As speculation drove land prices up, the towers climbed higher and higher, doubling the city's office space between 1920 and 1935. The Chrysler Building (1930) was, at 1,048 feet, the tallest building in the world until it was surpassed by the Empire State Building (1,250 feet) only a few months later. In 1929, construction began on Rockefeller Center, a complex of nineteen commercial buildings, including the RCA Building and Radio City Music Hall—a city within a city. Margaret Bourke-White, Lewis W. Hine, and Berenice Abbott were commissioned to document the construction of these monumental structures, and their dramatic photographs attest to the optimism and ambition of the era.

From the window of their suite at the Shelton Hotel, Georgia O'Keeffe and Alfred Stieglitz documented the surrounding sea of rooftops and the glitter of the city by night. For photographers, painters, and printmakers alike, the soaring skyscraper and the city's distinctive skyline emerged as universally recognized icons of progress and modernity.

ALFRED STIEGLITZ, **From My Window at the Shelton—Southeast**, 1931

STUART DAVIS, **New York Mural**, 1932

JOHN MARIN, **Mid-Manhattan, No. 1**, 1932

WALKER EVANS, **Construction of Building**, c. 1928–29

LEWIS W. HINE, **Untitled**, 1930–31

WALKER EVANS, **Architectural Study with Crane**, c. 1928–29

LEWIS W. HINE, **View of New York City from Empire State Building, Looking South**, 1931

15 February 1930   17 March 1930   15 April 1930

1 July 1930

1 August 1930

THURMAN ROTAN, **Skyscrapers**, 1932

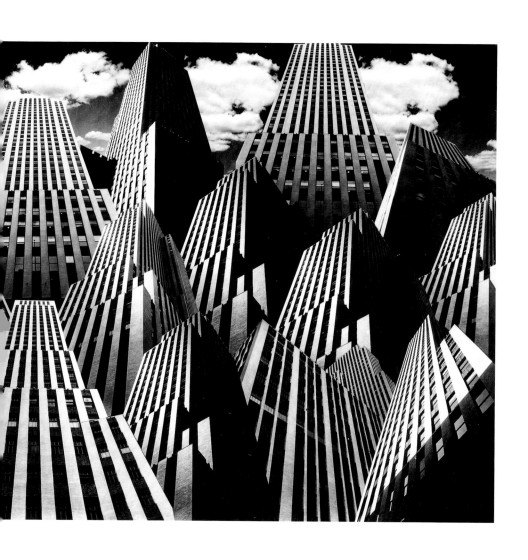

MARGARET BOURKE-WHITE, **Chrysler Building**, C. 1930

GORDON H. COSTER, **The Chrysler Building, New York City**, 1929

HOWARD COOK, **Times Square Sector**, 1930

ANSEL ADAMS,
**R.C.A. Building from Roof of
the Museum of Modern Art, New York City**, 1942

OWEN H. RAMSBURG,
Model of Rockefeller Center, early 1930s

WALKER EVANS, **New York City (Sign)**, 1928–29

BERENICE ABBOTT, **The Night View**, c. 1936

WHARTON ESHERICK, **Of a Great City**, 1927

HOWARD COOK, **Skyscraper**, 1928

THE LURE OF NEW YORK

E.B. WHITE

The inquiring photographer of the *Daily News* stopped six people the other day and asked them why they loved New York. He got six different answers. One lady said she loved New York because it was vibrant. One man said he loved it because business was good here. These replies made us think of the fine, clear answer which a friend of ours, a Greek shoeblack, once gave to the same question. This gentleman had got sick of New York, had wearied of his little shoe-and-hat parlor with its smell of polish and gasoline, and had gone back to his native island of Keos, where, he told us, he would just swim and fish and lie in the grass while beautiful girls fed him fruit. He was back in town in about four months. We asked him what there was about this city, what mysterious property, that had lured him back from the heaven that was Keos. He thought for a minute. Then he said, "In New York you can buy things so late at night."

From *The New Yorker*

1929 – 1939

LIFE IN THE METROPOLIS

ON OCTOBER 29, 1929, the Roaring Twenties came to a screeching halt, and the country slid into a deep economic depression. As the stock market crashed, the shining skyscrapers, newly completed, stood in sharp contrast to life in the city's tenements and streets.

The Great Depression had a profound effect on New York's artistic community. Abandoning their pursuit of new and modern means of expression, many artists adopted a more accessible, realist approach. They also turned from the towers of commerce to a new subject: the daily activities of the city's inhabitants. Reginald Marsh was prominent among these artists, depicting the city's bawdy cabarets and grim bread lines in somberly colored paintings and sober black-and-white prints. Many artists aligned themselves with the political left and promoted social consciousness through such organizations as the John Reed Club and the Artists' Union.

ISAAC SOYER, **Employment Agency**, 1937

REGINALD MARSH, **Lunch**, 1927

REGINALD MARSH, **Star Burlesk**, 1933

REGINALD MARSH, **Irving Place
Burlesk**, 1930

REGINALD MARSH, **Minsky's New Gotham Chorus**, 1936

EDWARD HOPPER, **Apartment Houses, Harlem River**, c. 1930

LOUIS LOZOWICK, **Excavation**, 1930

STUART DAVIS, **Two Figures and El**, 1931

EDWARD HOPPER, **The City**, 1927

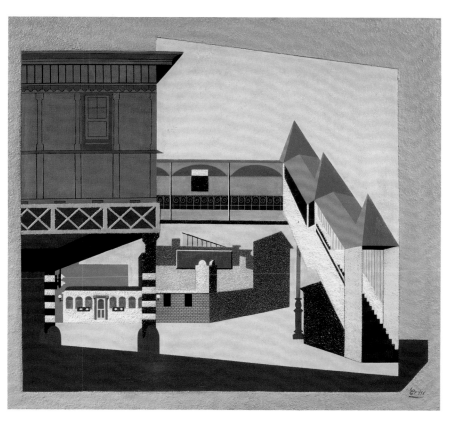

FRANCIS CRISS, **Sixth Avenue El**, c. 1937

KENNETH HAYES MILLER, **Shopper**, 1928

KENNETH HAYES MILLER, **Department Store**, 1930

TONI FRISSELL, **Woman in Front of ONE WAY Sign**, 1936

TONI FRISSELL, **Portrait of Lynn and Alfred Lunt
(A Christmas Card)**, 1936

TONI FRISSELL, **Woman with Black Coat**, 1939

THE HEART OF HARLEM

LANGSTON HUGHES

The buildings in Harlem are brick and stone
And the streets are long and wide,
But Harlem's much more than these alone,
Harlem is what's inside—
It's a song with a minor refrain,
It's a dream you keep dreaming again.
It's a tear you turn into a smile.
It's the sunrise you know is coming after a while.
It's the shoes that you get half-soled twice.
It's the kid you hope will grow up nice.
It's the hand that's working all day long.
It's a prayer that keeps you going along—
    That's the Heart of Harlem!

It's Joe Louis and Dr. W.E.B.,
A stevedore, a porter, Marian Anderson, and me.
It's Father Divine and the music of Earl Hines,
Adam Powell in Congress, our drivers on bus lines.
It's Dorothy Maynor and it's Billie Holiday,
The lectures at the Schomburg and the Apollo down
    the way.
It's Father Shelton Bishop and shouting Mother Horne.
It's the Rennie and the Savoy where new dances are
    born.
It's Canada Lee's penthouse at Five-Fifty-Five.
It's Small's Paradise and Jimmy's little dive.
It's 409 Edgecombe or a cold-water walk-up flat—
But it's where I live and it's where my love is at
    Deep in the Heart of Harlem!

It's the pride all Americans know.
It's the faith God gave us long ago.
It's the strength to make our dreams come true.
It's a feeling warm and friendly given to you.
It's that girl with the rhythmical walk.
It's my boy with the jive in his talk.
It's the man with the muscles of steel.
It's the right to be free a people never will yield.
A dream...a song...half-soled shoes...dancing shoes
A tear...a smile...the blues...sometimes the
    blues
Mixed with the memory...and forgiveness...of our
    wrong.
But more than that, it's freedom—
Guarded for the kids who came along—
    Folks, that's the Heart of Harlem!

1939 – 1945

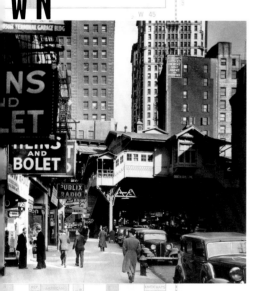

AS WORLD WAR II raged in Europe, artists in New York turned to the street life and night life of the city. William Johnson's jitterbuggers and Lisette Model's bar-goers document the city's exuberant entertainment world, which flourished throughout the war years. Ben Shahn's and Helen Levitt's depictions of children at play remind us that life went on despite the violence and tragedy overseas and the personal losses at home.

At the same time, there was a persistent mood of alienation and despair—here captured by Edward Hopper's *Office at Night* and in Willem de Kooning's eerie drawing *Manikins*. As the tabloid industry expanded, Weegee (Arthur Fellig) elevated the news photo to a new genre of photography with his nocturnal crime scenes.

WILLIAM H. JOHNSON, **Street Life, Harlem**, c. 1939–40

WILLIAM H. JOHNSON,
Jitterbugs VI, 1941–42

WILLIAM H. JOHNSON, **Moon Over Harlem**, c. 1943–44

WEEGEE, **Untitled (New York City Lightning Bolt)**, c. 1945

WEEGEE, **Untitled (I Cried When I Took This Picture)**, c. 1940

WEEGEE, **Untitled (Dead Man in Street)**, c. 1950

WEEGEE, **The Critic**, c. 1943

HELEN LEVITT, **Street Drawing**, C. 1940

EDWARD HOPPER, Study for **Office at Night**, 1940

WILLEM DE KOONING, **Manikins**, c. 1942

HONORE SHARRER, **Workers and Paintings**, 1943

LISETTE MODEL, **Sammy's, New York**, c. 1940–44

LISETTE MODEL, **Sammy's, New York**, c. 1940–44

JOSEPH DELANEY, **Street Festival, NYC**, 1940

1945

AN AGE C

THE GROUP

MARY MCCARTHY

They were in the throes of discovering
New York, imagine it, when some of
them had actually lived here all their
lives, in tiresome Georgian houses full of
waste space in the Eighties or Park
Avenue apartment buildings, and they
delighted in such out-of-the-way corners
as this, with its greenery and Quaker
meeting-house in red brick, polished
brass, and white trim next to the wine-
purple Episcopal church—on Sundays,
they walked with their beaux across
Brooklyn Bridge and poked into the
sleepy Heights section of Brooklyn; they
explored residential Murray Hill and
quaint MacDougal Alley and Patchin
Place and Washington Mews with all the
artists' studios; they loved the Plaza
Hotel and the fountain there and
the green mansarding of the Savoy Plaza
and the row of horsedrawn hacks
and elderly coachmen, waiting, as in
a French *place*, to tempt them to a
twilight right through Central Park.

060

PTIMISM

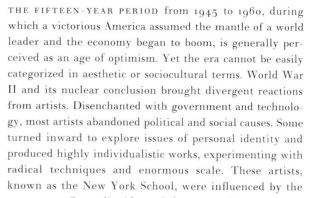

THE FIFTEEN-YEAR PERIOD from 1945 to 1960, during which a victorious America assumed the mantle of a world leader and the economy began to boom, is generally perceived as an age of optimism. Yet the era cannot be easily categorized in aesthetic or sociocultural terms. World War II and its nuclear conclusion brought divergent reactions from artists. Disenchanted with government and technology, most artists abandoned political and social causes. Some turned inward to explore issues of personal identity and produced highly individualistic works, experimenting with radical techniques and enormous scale. These artists, known as the New York School, were influenced by the Surrealist ideas of the recent European émigrés, absorbing their interest in mythology and Jungian psychology.

Other artists looked to the urban environment for subject matter. Influenced by Piet Mondrian's theories on art, Leon Polk Smith turned the pattern of the city's gridded streets into abstract, geometric canvases. Others, such as Ellsworth Kelly, Franz Kline, and Aaron Siskind, abstracted the textures, signs, walls, and fragments of the city.

By 1950, despite the country's postwar prosperity, the cold war and the threat of Russia's nuclear power was creating an atmosphere of anxiety and suspicion. In that year, Senator Joseph McCarthy initiated a nationwide "red scare," in which many intellectuals and artists aligned with the political left became targets of a witch hunt. A sense of fear and alienation from American life began to pervade the art community. Looking at the vast New York subway system, George Tooker did not see, as had earlier generations, an icon of speed or urban technology, but rather human despair born of emotional isolation—a true "lonely crowd." The 1950s may have been an age of optimism on many levels, but some artists, plumbing the depths of the national psyche, saw a dark, disturbing undercurrent.

AARON SISKIND, **New York 7**, 1950

WILLEM DE KOONING, **Sagamore**, 1955

BEAUFORD DELANEY, **Washington Square**, 1952

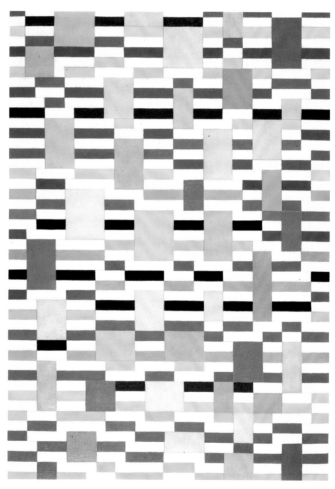

LEON POLK SMITH, **N.Y. City**, 1945

RUDY BURCKHARDT, **Astor Place**, 1948

RUDY BURCKHARDT, **Chelseascape I**, c. 1947

RUDY BURCKHARDT, **A View from Astoria**, 1940

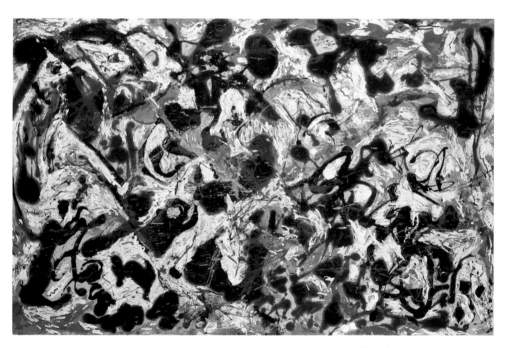

JACKSON POLLOCK, **Search**, 1955

WILLIAM KLEIN, **Selwyn New York**, 1955

NORMAN LEWIS, **Harlem Turns White**, 1955

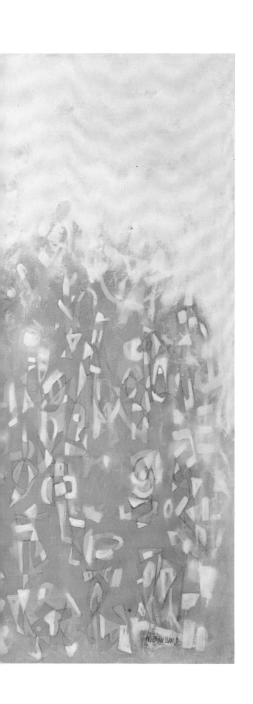

DIANE ARBUS, **Andrew
Ratoucheff, actor, 54, in his
Manhattan rooming
house following a late-show performance of his specialty:
imitations of Marilyn Monroe and of Maurice Chevalier singing
"Valentina",** 1960

DIANE ARBUS, **Carroll Baker on screen in "Baby Doll"**, 1956

ELLSWORTH KELLY, **New York, N.Y.**, 1957

Dimensions are in inches, followed by centimeters; height precedes width precedes depth.

WORKS IN THE EXHIBITION

As of May 20, 1996

BERENICE ABBOTT
(1898–1991)

Rockefeller Center, New York City, 1932
Gelatin silver print, 16½ x 13⁹⁄₁₆ (42.3 x 34.8)
Centre Canadien d'Architecture/Canadian Centre for Architecture, Montreal

Pennsylvania Station, 1936
Gelatin silver print, 9⅞ x 7⅞ (25.1 x 20)
Museum of the City of New York; Gift of the Works Projects Administration

Pennsylvania Station, 1936
Gelatin silver print, 9½ x 7½ (24.1 x 19.1)
Museum of the City of New York

The Night View, c. 1936 (1974 print)
Gelatin silver print, 13⅞ x 11 (35.2 x 27.9)
Museum of the City of New York; Gift of Mr. Todd Watts

ANSEL ADAMS
(1902–1984)

R.C.A. Building from Roof of the Museum of Modern Art, New York City, 1942
Gelatin silver print, 12¹³⁄₁₆ x 9¹⁵⁄₁₆ (32.8 x 25.5)
Center for Creative Photography, The University of Arizona, Tucson

DIANE ARBUS
(1923–1971)

Carroll Baker on screen in "Baby Doll", 1956
Gelatin silver print, 7 x 10¹⁵⁄₁₆ (17.8 x 27.8)
Whitney Museum of American Art, New York; Purchase, with funds from the Photography Committee 95.4

Andrew Ratoucheff, actor, 54, in his Manhattan rooming house following a late-show performance of his specialty: imitations of Marilyn Monroe and of Maurice Chevalier singing "Valentina", 1960
Published in "The Vertical Journey: Six Movements of a Moment Within the Heart of the City," *Esquire*, July 1960
Gelatin silver print, 9⅝ x 5¾ (2.1 x 14.7)
Spencer Museum of Art, The University of Kansas, Lawrence; Gift of Esquire, Inc.

Flora Knapp Dickinson, Honorary Regent of the Washington Heights Chapter of the Daughters of the American Revolution, 1960
Published in "The Vertical Journey: Six Movements of a Moment Within the Heart of the City," *Esquire*, July 1960
Gelatin silver print, 8⅞ x 5¹⁵⁄₁₆ (22.8 x 15.3)
Spencer Museum of Art, The University of Kansas, Lawrence; Gift of Esquire, Inc.

Hezekiah Trambles, "The Jungle Creep," performs five times a day at Hubert's Museum, 42nd & Broadway, Times Square, 1960
Published in "The Vertical Journey: Six Movements of a Moment Within the Heart of the City," *Esquire*, July 1960
Gelatin silver print, 9 x 5¹⁵⁄₁₆ (23 x 15.2)
Spencer Museum of Art, The University of Kansas, Lawrence; Gift of Esquire, Inc.

Mrs. Dagmar Patino, photographed at the Grand Opera Ball benefiting Boystown of Italy, Sheraton East Hotel, 1960
Published in "The Vertical Journey: Six Movements of a Moment Within the Heart of the City," *Esquire*, July 1960
Gelatin silver print, 8¾ x 5¹¹⁄₁₆ (22.5 x 14.6)
Spencer Museum of Art, The University of Kansas, Lawrence; Gift of Esquire, Inc.

Person Unknown, City Morgue, Bellevue Hospital, 1960
Published in "The Vertical Journey: Six Movements of a Moment Within the Heart of the City," *Esquire*, July 1960
Gelatin silver print, 9⅜ x 5 (24 x 15.3)
Spencer Museum of Art, The University of Kansas, Lawrence; Gift of Esquire, Inc.

Walter L. Gregory, also known as The Mad Man from Massachusetts, photographed in the city room of "The Bowery News", 1960
Published in "The Vertical Journey: Six Movements of a Moment Within the Heart of the City," *Esquire*, July 1960
Gelatin silver print, 9¹⁄₁₆ x 6⅛ (23.2 x 15.7)
Spencer Museum of Art, The University of Kansas, Lawrence; Gift of Esquire, Inc.

GEORGE C. AULT
(1891–1948)

From Brooklyn Heights, 1925
Oil on canvas, 30 x 20 (76.2 x 50.8)
The Newark Museum, New Jersey; Purchase 1928, The General Fund

Hudson Street, 1932
Oil on canvas, 24 x 20 (61 x 50.8)
Whitney Museum of American Art, New York; Purchase 33.40

ALICE AUSTEN
(1866–1952)

Ragpickers and Handcarts, 23rd Street and Third Ave., N.Y., c. 1896
Gelatin silver print, 3¾ x 4⁹⁄₁₆ (9.5 x 11.6)
Alice Austen Collection, Staten Island Historical Society, New York

GEORGE BELLOWS
(1882–1925)

Pennsylvania Station Excavation, 1909
Oil on canvas, 31¼ x 38¼ (79.4 x 97.2)
The Brooklyn Museum, New York

In the Park, 1916
Lithograph: sheet, 21¼ x 27¹⁄₁₆ (54 x 68.7); image, 16 x 21⅛ (40.6 x 53.7)
Whitney Museum of American Art, New York; Purchase, with funds from the Vain and Harry Fish Foundation 85.32

ISABEL BISHOP
(1902–1988)

On the Street, 1931
Etching: sheet, 7⅛ x 14¹⁵⁄₁₆
(18.1 x 37.9); plate, 4¹⁵⁄₁₆ x 10¹³⁄₁₆
(12.5 x 27.5)
Whitney Museum of American Art,
New York; Purchase 34.34

ILYA BOLOTOWSKY
(1907–1981)

City Rectangle, 1948
Oil on canvas, 34 x 26 (86.4 x 66)
Joan T. Washburn Gallery,
New York

MARGARET BOURKE-WHITE
(1904–1971)

Chrysler Building, 1929–30
Gelatin silver print, 13½ x 9⅜
(34.3 x 23.8)
Syracuse University Library,
Department of Special Collections,
New York

Chrysler Building, c. 1930
Gelatin silver print, 13⅛ x 9¹⁄₁₆
(33.3 x 23)
Syracuse University Library,
Department of Special Collections,
New York

Senator Wagner, 1938
Gelatin silver print
LIFE Magazine, New York

RUDY BURCKHARDT
(B. 1914)

A View from Astoria, 1940
Gelatin silver print, 7¾ x 11⅛
(19.7 x 28.3)
Tibor de Nagy Gallery, New York

Chelseascape I, c. 1947
Gelatin silver print, 8¾ x 11¼
(22.2 x 28.6)
Tibor de Nagy Gallery, New York

Astor Place, 1948
Gelatin silver print, 9¾ x 10
(24.8 x 25.4)
Tibor de Nagy Gallery, New York

MINNA WRIGHT CITRON
(1896–1991)

Staten Island Ferry, 1937
Oil on masonite, 25¼ x 16⅜
(64.1 x 41.6)
The Newark Museum; Purchase,
1939, Felix Fuld Bequest Fund

ALVIN LANGDON COBURN
(1882–1966)

The Flat-Iron Building, 1909
Gum platinum print, 11⅛ x 8⅛
(28.3 x 20.6)
Janet Lehr, Inc., New York

Brooklyn Bridge, New York, 1911
Platinum print, 12¼ x 15¾
(31.1 x 40)
Janet Lehr, Inc., New York

The Octopus, 1912 (1947 print)
Gelatin silver print, 8 x 5⅞
(20.5 x 15.1)
George Eastman House, Rochester;
Gift of The Museum of Modern Art

Ferryboat, New York Harbor, 1910
Platinum print, 8³⁄₁₆ x 8
(20.8 x 20.3)
Janet Lehr, Inc., New York

HOWARD COOK
(1901–1980)

Skyscraper, 1928
Woodcut: sheet, 19¼ x 9⁷⁄₁₆
(48.9 x 24); image, 17¹⁵⁄₁₆ x 8⅝
(45.6 x 21.9)
Whitney Museum of American
Art, New York

Lower Manhattan, 1930
Lithograph: sheet, 15⅝ x 11¼ (39.7
x 28.6); image, 14 x 10 (35.6 x 25.4)
Whitney Museum of American
Art, New York; Gift of Mr.
and Mrs. R. Gray Winnan 72.18

Times Square Sector, 1930
Etching: sheet, 13⅞ x 11½ (35.2 x
29.2); plate, 11¹³⁄₁₆ x 9⅞ (30 x 25.1)
Whitney Museum of American
Art, New York; Gift of Associated
American Artists 77.17

The West Side, New York, 1931
Etching and aquatint: sheet,
11½ x 15¾ (29.2 x 40);
plate, 6¹¹⁄₁₆ x 12⁷⁄₁₆ (17 x 31.6)
Whitney Museum of American
Art, New York; Gift of Mr.
and Mrs. Michael Irving 78.82

GORDON H. COSTER
(1903–1988)

The Chrysler Building, New York City, 1929
Brown-toned gelatin silver print
mounted on board, 13⁷⁄₁₆ x 10⁷⁄₁₆
(34.5 x 26.7)
Centre Canadien d'Architecture/
Canadian Centre for Architecture,
Montreal

FRANCIS CRISS
(1901–1973)

Sixth Avenue El, c. 1937
Oil on canvas, 36 x 41½
(91.4 x 105.4)
Whitney Museum of American
Art, New York; Purchase,
with funds from the Felicia Meyer
Marsh Purchase Fund 82.1

STUART DAVIS
(1892–1964)

Sixth Avenue El, 1931
Lithograph: sheet, 15⅞ x 21⅛
(40.3 x 53.7); image, 11¹⁵⁄₁₆ x 18
(30.3 x 45.7)
Whitney Museum of American Art,
New York; Purchase, with
funds from Mr. and Mrs. Samuel
M. Kootz 77.74

Two Figures and El, 1931
Lithograph: sheet, 20⅛ x 26 (51.1 x
66); image, 11 x 15 (27.9 x 38.1)
Whitney Museum of American Art,
New York; Purchase, and gift
of Mr. and Mrs. Michael Irving, by
exchange 77.13

New York Mural, 1932
Oil on canvas, 84 x 38 (213.4 x 96.5)
Norton Museum of Art, West
Palm Beach, Florida

WILLEM DE KOONING
(B. 1904)

Manikins, c. 1942
Graphite on paper, 13½ x 16¼
(34.3 x 41.3) sight
Whitney Museum of American Art,
New York; Purchase, with funds
from the Grace Belt Endowed
Purchase Fund, the Burroughs
Wellcome Purchase Fund,
The Norman and Rosita Winston
Foundation, Inc., the Drawing
Committee, and an anonymous
donor 84.5

Sagamore, 1955
Oil on canvas, 22½ x 27 (57.2 x 68.6)
Collection of Dr. and Mrs. Sydney
Clyman

BEAUFORD DELANEY
(1901–1979)

Washington Square, 1952
Oil on canvas, 40 x 60 (101.6 x 152.4)
Greenville County Museum of Art, South Carolina; Museum purchase with funds from the Arthur and Holly Magill Fund; courtesy Michael Rosenfeld Gallery, New York

JOSEPH DELANEY
(1904–1991)

Street Festival, NYC, 1940
Oil on canvas, 30 x 24 (76.2 x 61)
Collection of John and Norma Thompson; courtesy Michael Rosenfeld Gallery, New York

PRESTON DICKINSON
(1889–1930)

Industry, c. 1923
Oil on canvas, 30 x 24¼ (76.2 x 61.6)
Whitney Museum of American Art, New York; Gift of Gertrude Vanderbilt Whitney 31.173

ELSIE DRIGGS
(1898–1992)

Queensborough Bridge, 1927
Oil on canvas, 40¼ x 30¼ (102.2 x 76.8)
The Montclair Art Museum, New Jersey; Museum Purchase, Florence O.R. Lang Fund

WILL EISNER
(B. 1917)

Life Below, February 22, 1948
Ink on board, 16½ x 11 (41.9 x 27.9)
Collection of the artist

WHARTON ESHERICK
(1887–1970)

Of a Great City, 1927
Wood engraving: sheet, 17$^{13}/_{16}$ x 12$^{7}/_{16}$ (45.2 x 31.6); image, 9⅞ x 6$^{5}/_{16}$ (25.1 x 16)
Whitney Museum of American Art, New York

WALKER EVANS
(1903–1975)

Untitled, c. 1928
Gelatin silver print, 1½ x 2½ (3.8 x 6.4)
The Museum of Modern Art, New York; Gift of Dr. Iago Galdston

Untitled, c. 1928
Gelatin silver print, 2⅜ x 3⅛ (6 x 7.9)
The Museum of Modern Art, New York; Gift of Dr. Iago Galdston

Untitled, c. 1928
Gelatin silver print, 2½ x 1½ (6.4 x 3.8)
The Museum of Modern Art, New York; Gift of Dr. Iago Galdston

Untitled, c. 1928
Gelatin silver print, 2½ x 1½ (6.4 x 3.8)
The Museum of Modern Art, New York; Gift of Dr. Iago Galdston

Untitled, c. 1928
Gelatin silver print, 1½ x 2½ (3.8 x 6.4)
The Museum of Modern Art, New York; Gift of Dr. Iago Galdston

Broadway Composition, 1928–29
Gelatin silver print, 10 x 8 (25.4 x 20.3)
Collection of Alan, Gloria, and Stacey Siegel; courtesy Bonni Benrubi Gallery, New York

New York City (Sign), 1928–29
Gelatin silver print, 9 x 6 (22.9 x 15.2)
Collection of Howard Greenberg

Architectural Study with Crane, c. 1928–29
Gelatin silver print, 2½ x 1⅝ (6.4 x 4.1)
Howard Greenberg Gallery, New York

Construction of Building, c. 1928–29
Gelatin silver print, 1⅝ x 2½ (4.1 x 6.4)
Howard Greenberg Gallery, New York

Brooklyn Bridge, New York, 1929
Gelatin silver print on postcard stock, 1½ x 2⅞ (3.8 x 7.3)
Howard Greenberg Gallery, New York

Subway Portrait, 1938–41
Gelatin silver print, 7 x 9$^{15}/_{16}$ (17.7 x 25.2)
National Gallery of Art, Washington, D.C.; Gift of Mr. and Mrs. Harry H. Lunn, Jr. in honor of Jacob Kainen and in Honor of the 50th Anniversary of the National Gallery of Art

Subway Portrait, 1938–41
Gelatin silver print, 5$^{3}/_{16}$ x 5$^{15}/_{16}$ (13.2 x 15.1)
National Gallery of Art, Washington, D.C.; Gift of Kent and Marcia Minichiello, in Honor of the 50th Anniversary of the National Gallery of Art

Subway Portrait, 1941
Gelatin silver print, 8¼ x 7½ (21 x 19.1)
National Gallery of Art, Washington, D.C.; Gift of Kent and Marcia Minichiello, in Honor of the 50th Anniversary of the National Gallery of Art

Subway Portrait, 1941
Gelatin silver print, 10$^{13}/_{16}$ x 8$^{7}/_{16}$ (27.5 x 21.4)
National Gallery of Art, Washington, D.C.; Gift of Kent and Marcia Minichiello, in Honor of the 50th Anniversary of the National Gallery of Art

LOUIS FAURER
(B. 1916)

Looking Toward RCA Building at Rockefeller Center, New York City, 1949
Gelatin silver print, 14 x 11 (35.6 x 27.9)
Deborah Bell, New York

Construction Site, Madison Avenue, Looking Toward Rockefeller Center, New York City, c. 1949
Gelatin silver print, 14 x 11 (35.6 x 27.9)
Deborah Bell, New York

Central Park Looking Towards (Mall) Lake, New York City, 1960
Gelatin silver print, 12½ x 10¾ (31.8 x 27.3)
Howard Greenberg Gallery, New York

HUGH FERRISS
(B. 1889)

The Shelton Hotel, 1927
Crayon on paper on board, 18 x 13½ (44.7 x 34.3)
Avery Library, Columbia University, New York

137

WILLIAM H. JOHNSON
(1901–1970)

Street Life, Harlem, c. 1939–40
Oil on plywood, 45¾ x 38⅝
(116 x 98)
National Museum of American Art,
Smithsonian Institution,
Washington, D.C.; Gift of the
Harmon Foundation

Jitterbugs VI, 1941–42
Color serigraph, 17⅜ x 11¼
(44.1 x 28.6)
Whitney Museum of American Art,
New York; Purchase, with funds
from the Print Committee 95.54

Blind Singer, c. 1942
Color serigraph, 17½ x 11⁹/₁₆
(44.5 x 29.4)
Whitney Museum of American Art,
New York; Purchase, with funds
from the Print Committee 95.53

Moon Over Harlem, c. 1943–44
Oil on plywood, 28½ x 35¾
(72.4 x 90.8)
National Museum of American Art,
Smithsonian Institution,
Washington, D.C.; Gift of the
Harmon Foundation

ELLSWORTH KELLY
(B. 1923)

New York, N.Y., 1957
Oil on canvas, 73¾ x 90
(187.3 x 228.6)
Albright-Knox Art Gallery, Buffalo,
New York; Gift of Seymour H.
Knox, 1959

WILLIAM KLEIN
(B. 1928)

Martian, Macy's Parade, 1954
Gelatin silver print, 10¼ x 13¼
(26 x 33.7)
Howard Greenberg Gallery,
New York

Pigeons, Herald Square, 1954
Gelatin silver print, 11¹⁵/₁₆ x 15¹⁵/₁₆
(30.3 x 40.5)
Whitney Museum of American Art,
New York; Gift of Virginia
Zabriskie 91.100.6

Stickball Dance—New York, 1954
Gelatin silver print, 15⅞ x 19¹⁵/₁₆
(40.3 x 50.6)
Whitney Museum of American Art,
New York; Gift of Virginia
Zabriskie 91.100.8

Car Under El, New York, 1955
Gelatin silver print, 14 x 11
(35.6 x 27.9)
Howard Greenberg Gallery,
New York

Elsa Maxwell's Toy Ball, New York, 1955
Gelatin silver print, 8½ x 11½
(21.6 x 29.2)
Howard Greenberg Gallery,
New York

$1.50, Cashier, 42nd Street, 1955
Gelatin silver print, 10¾ x 13¾
(27.3 x 34.9)
Howard Greenberg Gallery,
New York

Selwyn New York, 1955
Gelatin silver print, 12 x 9½
(30.5 x 24.1)
Whitney Museum of American Art,
New York; Purchase, with funds
from the Photography Committee
96.64

FRANZ KLINE
(1910–1962)

Untitled (Study for **Wanamaker
Block**), c. 1954
Ink on paper, 17 x 16 (43.2 x 40.6)
Collection of Mr. and Mrs.
Donald Garlikov

Untitled, 1960
Oil on canvas, 116¼ x 39¼
(295.3 x 99.7)
Collection of Jeffrey E. Epstein

JACOB LAWRENCE
(B. 1917)

**BOOTLEG WHISKEY: You can buy
bootleg whiskey for twenty-five cents
a quart**, 1943
Gouache on paper, 15½ x 22½
(39.4 x 57.2)
Portland Art Museum, Oregon;
Winslow B. Ayer Fund

**FREE CLINIC: Harlem Hospital's free
clinic is crowded with patients every
morning and evening**, 1943
Gouache on paper, 14⅛ x 21¼
(35.9 x 54)
Portland Art Museum, Oregon;
Winslow B. Ayer Fund

HARLEM: And Harlem society looks on, 1943
Gouache on paper, 15 x 21¾
(38.1 x 55.3)
Portland Art Museum, Oregon;
Winslow B. Ayer Fund

ERNEST LAWSON
(1873–1939)

Winter on the River, 1907
Oil on canvas, 33 x 40 (83.8 x 101.6)
Whitney Museum of American
Art, New York; Gift of Gertrude
Vanderbilt Whitney 31.280

High Bridge—Early Moon, c. 1910
Oil on canvas mounted on panel,
20 x 24 (50.8 x 61)
The Phillips Collection,
Washington, D.C.

HELEN LEVITT
(B. 1913)

Street Drawing, c. 1940
Gelatin silver print, 13¹⁵/₁₆ x 10⅞
(35.4 x 27.6)
Whitney Museum of American Art,
New York; Gift of Lilyan S. and
Toby Miller 94.167

NORMAN LEWIS
(1909–1979)

Harlem Turns White, 1955
Oil on canvas, 50 x 64 (127 x 162.6)
Michael Rosenfeld Gallery,
New York

LOUIS LOZOWICK
(1892–1973)

New York, 1925
Lithograph: sheet, 15⅛ x 11⅜
(38.4 x 28.9); image, 11⁹/₁₆ x 9
(29.4 x 22.9)
Whitney Museum of American Art,
New York; Purchase, with funds
from the John I.H. Baur Purchase
Fund 77.12

Coney Island, 1929
Lithograph: sheet, 15⅞ x 11⁷/₁₆
(40.3 x 29.1); image, 12¾ x 8½
(32.4 x 21.6)
Whitney Museum of American Art,
New York; Purchase, with funds
from Lily Auchincloss 77.18

Excavation, 1930
Lithograph: sheet, 18¹³/₁₆ x 13¾
(47.8 x 34.9); image, 15⅞ x 6¼
(40.3 x 15.9)
Whitney Museum of American Art,
New York; Purchase 31.945

Subway Construction, 1931
Lithograph: sheet, 11 5/16 x 15 7/8 (28.7 x 40.3); image, 6 5/8 x 13 1/16 (16.8 x 33.2)
Whitney Museum of American Art, New York; Purchase, with funds from Philip Morris Incorporated 77.8

GEORGE LUKS
(1867–1933)

Houston Street, 1917
Oil on canvas, 24 x 42 (61 x 106.7)
The Saint Louis Art Museum, Missouri; Bequest of Marie Setz Hertslet

MAN RAY
(1890–1977)

New York 17, 1917
Construction of chrome-plated bronze and brass and painted brass vise, 17 3/8 x 9 1/4 x 9 1/4 (44.1 x 23.5 x 23.5)
Hirshhorn Museum and Sculpture Garden, Smithsonian Institution, Washington, D.C.; Gift of Joseph H. Hirshhorn, 1972

JOHN MARIN
(1870–1953)

Downtown from River, 1910
Watercolor on paper, 14 x 17 (35.6 x 43.2)
Collection of Jules and Connie Kay

The Woolworth Building, 1913
Etching with drypoint: sheet, 16 13/16 x 14 1/16 (42.7 x 35.7); image, 12 7/8 x 10 3/8 (32.7 x 26.4)
Whitney Museum of American Art, New York; Gift of Gertrude Vanderbilt Whitney 31.776

Lower Manhattan (Composing Derived from Top of Woolworth), 1922
Watercolor and charcoal with paper cutout attached with thread, 21 5/8 x 26 7/8 (54.9 x 68.3)
The Museum of Modern Art, New York; Acquired through the Lillie P. Bliss Bequest

Street Crossing, New York, 1928
Watercolor on paper, 26 1/4 x 21 3/4 (66.7 x 55.2)
The Phillips Collection, Washington, D.C.

Broadway Night, 1929
Watercolor and charcoal on paper, 21 1/2 x 26 3/4 (54.6 x 67.9)
The Metropolitan Museum of Art, New York; Alfred Stieglitz Collection, 1949

Mid-Manhattan, No. 1, 1932
Oil on canvas, 28 x 22 (71.1 x 55.9)
Des Moines Art Center; Purchased with funds from the Coffin Fine Arts Trust, Nathan Emory Coffin Collection of the Des Moines Art Center

Region of Brooklyn Bridge Fantasy, 1932
Watercolor on paper, 18 3/4 x 22 1/4 (47.6 x 56.5)
Whitney Museum of American Art, New York; Purchase 49.8

REGINALD MARSH
(1898–1954)

Lunch, 1927
Oil on canvas, 24 x 36 (61 x 91.4)
Whitney Museum of American Art, New York; Felicia Meyer Marsh Bequest 80.31.3

People Seated and Standing in Subway, c. 1928
Oil on canvas, 36 x 48 (91.4 x 121.9)
Whitney Museum of American Art, New York; Felicia Meyer Marsh Bequest 80.31.8

The El, c. 1928
Oil on canvas, 30 x 40 (76.2 x 101.6)
Whitney Museum of American Art, New York; Felicia Meyer Marsh Bequest 80.31.9

Gaiety Burlesk, 1930
Etching: sheet, 15 1/2 x 13 1/8 (39.4 x 33.3); image, 11 7/8 x 9 3/4 (30.2 x 24.8)
Whitney Museum of American Art, New York; Original plate donated by William Benton 69.97.5

Irving Place Burlesk, 1930
Etching: sheet, 13 x 15 1/2 (33 x 39.4); image, 9 3/4 x 12 13/16 (24.8 x 32.5)
Whitney Museum of American Art, New York; Original plate donated by William Benton 69.97.4

Bread Line—No One Has Starved, 1932
Etching: sheet, 13 1/16 x 15 1/2 (33.2 x 39.4); image, 6 5/16 x 11 7/8 (16 x 30.2)
Whitney Museum of American Art, New York; Original plate donated by William Benton 69.97.10

Star Burlesk, 1933
Etching: sheet, 15 9/16 x 13 1/16 (39.5 x 33.2); image, 11 7/8 x 8 13/16 (30.2 x 22.4)
Whitney Museum of American Art, New York; Original plate donated by William Benton 69.97.12

Minsky's Chorus, 1935
Tempera on composition board, 38 x 44 (96.5 x 111.8)
Whitney Museum of American Art, New York; Partial and promised gift of Mr. and Mrs. Albert Hackett in honor of Edith and Lloyd Goodrich P.5.83

Minsky's New Gotham Chorus, 1936
Etching: sheet, 13 1/8 x 15 1/2 (33.3 x 39.4); image, 8 13/16 x 11 15/16
Whitney Museum of American Art, New York; Original plate donated by William Benton 69.97.18

JAN MATULKA
(1890–1972)

New York Evening, 1925
Lithograph: sheet, 14 7/16 x 19 1/2 (36.7 x 49.5); image, 14 7/16 x 19 1/2 (36.7 x 49.5)
Whitney Museum of American Art, New York; Purchase 77.9

KENNETH HAYES MILLER
(1876–1952)

Leaving the Shop, 1925
Etching: sheet, 9 9/16 x 12 5/16 (24.3 x 31.3); image, 7 15/16 x 9 7/8 (20.2 x 25.1)
Whitney Museum of American Art, New York; Purchase 31.790

Shopper, 1928
Oil on canvas, 41 x 33 (104.1 x 83.8)
Whitney Museum of American Art, New York; Purchase 31.305

Department Store, 1930
Etching: sheet, 10 3/16 x 7 3/16 (25.9 x 18.3); image, 6 15/16 x 4 15/16 (17.6 x 12.5)
Whitney Museum of American Art, New York; Purchase 31.792

On Fourteenth Street, 1932
Ink and crayon on paper, 12 x 15 (30.5 x 38.1)
Whitney Museum of American Art, New York; Purchase 45.20

LISETTE MODEL
(1906–1983)

Sammy's, New York, c. 1940–44
Gelatin silver print, 13 5/8 x 10 3/4 (34.3 x 27.6)
Gift of the Estate of Lisette Model, 1990, by direction of Joseph G. Blum, New York, through the American Friends of Canada, National Gallery of Canada, Ottawa

Sammy's, New York, c. 1940–44
Gelatin silver print, 10 7/16 x 13 5/16 (26.7 x 34.2)
National Gallery of Canada, Ottawa; Estate of Lisette Model

Sammy's, New York, c. 1940–44
Gelatin silver print, 19 11/16 x 15 11/16 (50.5 x 40.2)
Gift of the Estate of Lisette Model, 1990, by direction of Joseph G. Blum, New York, through the American Friends of Canada, National Gallery of Canada, Ottawa

Sammy's, New York, c. 1940–44
Gelatin silver print, 13 5/8 x 10 1/2 (34.9 x 26.9)
National Gallery of Canada, Ottawa

ARNOLD NEWMAN
(B. 1918)

Robert Moses standing with a panoramic view of midtown Manhattan behind, 1959
Gelatin silver print
Centre Canadien d'Architecture/ Canadian Centre for Architecture, Montreal

GEORGIA O'KEEFFE
(1887–1986)

East River, No. 3, 1926
Oil on canvas, 12 x 32 1/4 (30.5 x 81.9)
Frances Lehman Loeb Art Center, Vassar College, Poughkeepsie, New York

East River with Sun (East River, New York, from the 28th Story of the Shelton Hotel, Morning), 1926
Pastel on paper, 10 3/4 x 27 3/4 (27.3 x 70.5)
Private collection

East River, New York, No. 2, 1927
Pastel on paper, 10 3/4 x 28 (27.3 x 71.1)
Collection of Richard and Leah Waitzer

Radiator Building—Night, New York, 1927
Oil on canvas, 48 x 30 (121.9 x 76.2)
The Alfred Stieglitz Collection, Fisk University, Nashville

East River from the Shelton, 1927–28
Oil on canvas, 26 x 22 (66 x 55.9)
New Jersey State Museum Collection, Trenton; Purchased by The Association for the Arts of the New Jersey State Museum with a gift by Mary Lea Johnson

JACKSON POLLOCK
(1912–1956)

Composition with Red Strokes, 1950
Oil, enamel, and aluminum paint on canvas, 36 5/8 x 25 5/8 (93 x 65.1)
Private collection; courtesy Jason McCoy, Inc., New York

Search, 1955
Oil on canvas, 57 1/2 x 90 (146.1 x 228.6)
Private collection; courtesy Jason McCoy, Inc., New York

ROBERT RAUSCHENBERG
(B. 1925)

Studio Painting, 1960–61
Oil, fabric, paper, rope, metal pulley, clasps, stuffed canvas bag, and charcoal on canvas, 72 x 72 (183 x 183) overall
C&M Arts, New York

THURMAN ROTAN
(1903–1991)

Skyscrapers, 1932
Photomontage, 10 x 19 1/4 (25.4 x 48.9)
Keith de Lellis, New York

BEN SHAHN
(1898–1969)

Handball, 1939
Tempera, 22 1/4 x 31 1/4 (56.5 x 79.4)
The Museum of Modern Art, New York; Abby Aldrich Rockefeller Fund, 1940

HONORE SHARRER

Workers and Paintings, 1943
Oil on composition board, 11 5/8 x 37 (29.5 x 94)
The Museum of Modern Art, New York; Gift of Lincoln Kirstein, 1944

CHARLES SHEELER
(1883–1965)

New York, Buildings in Shadow, 1920
Gelatin silver print, 10 x 8 (25.4 x 20.3)
Museum of Fine Arts, Boston; Lane Collection

New York, Park Row Building, 1920
Gelatin silver print, 10 x 8 (25.4 x 20.3)
Museum of Fine Arts, Boston; Lane Collection

New York, Towards the Woolworth Building, 1920
Gelatin silver print, 10 x 8 (25.4 x 20.3)
Museum of Fine Arts, Boston; Lane Collection

New York, Broadway at Fortieth Street, c. 1920
Gelatin silver print, 10 x 8 (25.4 x 20.3)
Museum of Fine Arts, Boston; Lane Collection

MacDougal Alley, 1924
Oil on canvas, 23 7/8 x 18 1/8 (60.6 x 46)
Davison Art Center, Wesleyan University, Middletown, Connecticut

AARON SISKIND
(1903–1991)

Aquarium 6B, 1946
Gelatin silver print, 14 x 11 (35.6 x 27.9)
Robert Mann Gallery, New York

NY South Street, 3, 1947
Gelatin silver print, 11 x 14 (27.9 x 35.6)
Robert Mann Gallery, New York

New York 7, 1950
Gelatin silver print, 14 x 11 (35.6 x 27.9)
Whitney Museum of American Art, New York; Purchase, with funds from the Photography Committee 96.63

JOHN SLOAN
(1871–1951)

Roofs, Summer Night, 1906
Etching: sheet, 9 1/2 x 12 5/8 (24.1 x 32.1); image, 5 1/4 x 6 15/16 (24.1 x 32.1)
Whitney Museum of American Art, New York; Purchase 31.826

Night Windows, 1910
Etching: sheet, 9 7/16 x 12 11/16 (24 x 32.2); image, 5 1/4 x 6 7/8 (13.3 x 17.5)
Whitney Museum of American Art, New York; Purchase 31.832

LEON POLK SMITH
(B. 1906)

N.Y. City, 1945
Oil on canvas, 47 x 33 (119.4 x 83.8)
Whitney Museum of American Art, New York; 50th Anniversary of the Edward R. Downe, Jr. Purchase Fund and the National Endowment for the Arts 79.24

ISAAC SOYER
(1907–1981)

Employment Agency, 1937
Oil on canvas, 34 1/4 x 45 (87 x 114.3)
Whitney Museum of American Art, New York; Purchase 37.44

RAPHAEL SOYER
(1899–1987)

Office Girls, 1936
Oil on canvas, 26 x 24 (66 x 61)
Whitney Museum of American Art,
New York; Purchase 36.149

NILES SPENCER
(1893–1952)

Apartment Tower, 1944
Oil on canvas, 32 x 24 (81.3 x 61)
Whitney Museum of American Art,
New York; Gift of Mr. and Mrs.
Alan H. Temple 55.42

EDWARD STEICHEN
(1879–1973)

**Vionnet Model Imported by Saks-Fifth
Avenue**, 1925
Gelatin silver print, 10 x 8
(25.4 x 20.3)
Howard Greenberg Gallery,
New York

View into 40th Street at Night, 1925
Warm-toned gelatin bromide print,
9 x 7½ (22.9 x 19.1)
Private collection; courtesy
Fraenkel Gallery, San Francisco

The Maypole, 1932
Gelatin silver print, 13¼ x 10⁷⁄₁₆
(33.7 x 26.5)
The Museum of Modern Art,
New York; Gift of the photographer

JOSEPH STELLA
(1877–1946)

**The Brooklyn Bridge: Variation on an
Old Theme**, 1939
Oil on canvas, 70 x 42
(177.8 x 106.7)
Whitney Museum of American Art,
New York; Purchase 42.15

Sketch for **Brooklyn Bridge**, n.d.
Pastel on paper, 21 x 17½
(53.3 x 44.5)
Whitney Museum of American Art,
New York; Gift of Miss Rose Fried
52.36

FLORINE STETTHEIMER
(1871–1944)

Spring Sale at Bendel's, 1921
Oil on canvas, 50 x 40 (127 x 101.6)
Philadelphia Museum of Art;
Given by Miss Ettie Stettheimer

LOU STETTNER
(1871–1944)

Untitled (Pennsylvania Station, NYC),
c. 1958
Gelatin silver print, 14 x 11
(35.6 x 27.9)
Collection of Sondra Gilman
Gonzalez-Falla; courtesy
Bonni Benrubi Gallery, New York

Untitled (Pennsylvania Station, NYC),
c. 1958
Gelatin silver print, 14 x 11
(35.6 x 27.9)
Bonni Benrubi Gallery, New York

ALFRED STIEGLITZ
(1864–1946)

In the New York Central Yards, 1903
Gelatin silver print, 12⁵⁄₁₆ x 10⁵⁄₁₆
(31.3 x 26.2)
National Gallery of Art,
Washington, D.C.; Alfred Stieglitz
Collection

The City of Ambition, 1910
Photogravure, 13³⁄₈ x 10¼ (34 x 26)
National Gallery of Art,
Washington, D.C.; Alfred Stieglitz
Collection

**From the Back Window, 291—New York,
Winter**, 1915
Platinum print, 9⅜ x 7⅜
(23.8 x 18.7)
Private collection; courtesy
Fraenkel Gallery, San Francisco

**View from the Rear Window, Gallery
291 at Night**, 1915
Platinum print, 10 x 8 (25.4 x 20.3)
Williams College Museum of Art,
Williamstown, Massachusetts; Gift
of John H. Rhoades, Class of 1934

**View from the Rear Window, Gallery
291, Daytime**, 1915
Platinum print, 10 x 8 (25.4 x 20.3)
Williams College Museum of Art,
Williamstown, Massachusetts; Gift
of John H. Rhoades, Class of 1934

**From Room '3003'—The Shelton,
New York, Looking N.E.**, 1927
Gelatin silver print mounted
on paperboard, 10¹³⁄₁₆ x 8⁷⁄₁₆
(27.5 x 21.4)
National Gallery of Art,
Washington, D.C.; Alfred Stieglitz
Collection

**From My Window at the Shelton—
Southeast**, 1931
Gelatin silver print mounted on
paperboard, 7⅜ x 9⅜ (18.7 x 23.8)
National Gallery of Art,
Washington, D.C.; Alfred Stieglitz
Collection

From the Shelton, 1931
Gelatin silver print mounted on
paperboard, 9½ x 7½ (24.1 x 19.1)
National Gallery of Art,
Washington, D.C.; Alfred Stieglitz
Collection

**From An American Place Looking
Southwest**, 1932
Gelatin silver print, 9⁵⁄₁₆ x 7¹⁄₁₆
(23.7 x 17.9)
National Gallery of Art,
Washington, D.C., Alfred Stieglitz
Collection

PAUL STRAND
(1890–1976)

Wall Street, New York, 1915
Platinum palladium print,
11 x 13⅞ (27.9 x 35.2)
Whitney Museum of American Art,
New York; Gift of Michael
E. Hoffman in honor of Sondra
Gilman 91.102.2

The Court, New York, 1928
Gelatin silver print, 9⅞ x 7⅜
(25.1 x 18.7)
San Francisco Museum of Modern
Art

KARL STRUSS
(1886–1981)

Construction—"Excuse Me", 1911
Platinum print, 4⁵⁄₁₆ x 3¾ (11 x 9.5)
Amon Carter Museum, Fort Worth

Pennsylvania Station, New York, 1911
Platinum print, 4¹¹⁄₁₆ x 3¹¹⁄₁₆
(11.9 x 9.4)
Amon Carter Museum, Fort Worth

**Brooklyn Bridge from Ferry Slip, Late
Afternoon**, 1912
Platinum print, 4⅞ x 3¹¹⁄₁₆ (12.4 x 9.4)
Amon Carter Museum, Fort Worth

GEORGE TOOKER
(B. 1920)

The Subway, 1950
Egg tempera on composition board,
18⅛ x 36⅛ (46 x 91.8)
Whitney Museum of American Art,
New York; Purchase, with funds
from the Juliana Force Purchase
Award 50.23

Government Bureau, 1956
Egg tempera on wood, 19⅝ x 29⅝
(49.8 x 75.2)
The Metropolitan Museum of Art,
New York; George A. Hearn Fund

IRVING UNDERHILL, INC.
UNKNOWN PHOTOGRAPHER

Irving Trust Company Building Site,
15 February 1930
Gelatin silver print, flush-mounted
on linen, 13¼ x 10 (34 x 25.7)
Centre Canadien d'Architecture/
Canadian Centre for Architecture,
Montreal

Irving Trust Company Building Site,
17 March 1930
Gelatin silver print, flush-mounted
on linen, 13³⁄₁₆ x 10¹⁄₁₆ (33.9 x 25.8)
Centre Canadien d'Architecture/
Canadian Centre for Architecture,
Montreal

Irving Trust Company Building Site,
15 April 1930
Gelatin silver print, flush-mounted
on linen, 13⁵⁄₁₆ x 10 (34.1 x 25.7)
Centre Canadien d'Architecture/
Canadian Centre for Architecture,
Montreal

Irving Trust Company Building Site,
1 July 1930
Gelatin silver print, flush-mounted
on linen, 13³⁄₁₆ x 10 (33.8 x 25.7)
Centre Canadien d'Architecture/
Canadian Centre for Architecture,
Montreal

Irving Trust Company Building Site,
1 August 1930
Gelatin silver print, flush-mounted
on linen, 13³⁄₁₆ x 10¹⁄₁₆ (33.8 x 25.8)
Centre Canadien d'Architecture/
Canadian Centre for Architecture,
Montreal

JAMES VAN DER ZEE
(1886–1983)

Abbyseyna [sic] Church, 140 Street,
New York City, 1927
Gelatin silver print, 7½ x 9½
(19.1 x 24.1)
Howard Greenberg Gallery,
New York

ABRAHAM WALKOWITZ
(1880–1965)

Cityscape, c. 1915
Oil on canvas, 25 x 18 (63.5 x 45.7)
Whitney Museum of American Art,
New York; Purchase,
with funds from Philip Morris
Incorporated 76.11

MAX WEBER
(1881–1961)

New York Department Store (An Idea of a
Modern Department Store), 1915
Oil on canvas, 46⅜ x 31 (117.8 x 78.7)
The Detroit Institute of Arts,
Founder Society Purchase, Mr. and
Mrs. Walter Buhl Ford, II Fund

WEEGEE (ARTHUR FELLIG)
(1899–1968)

Untitled (I Cried When I Took This Picture),
c. 1940
Gelatin silver print, 10¹⁵⁄₁₆ x 13⅞
(27.8 x 35.2)
Whitney Museum of American Art,
New York; Gift of Denise Rich
96.90.5

The Critic, c. 1943
Gelatin silver print, 11 x 13⅞
(27.9 x 35.2)
Whitney Museum of American Art,
New York; Gift of Denise Rich
96.90.2

Untitled (New York City Lightning Bolt),
c. 1945
Gelatin silver print, 13¹⁵⁄₁₆ x 11
(35.4 x 27.9)
Whitney Museum of American Art,
New York; Gift of Denise Rich
96.90.14

Untitled (Dead Man in Street), c. 1950
Gelatin silver print, 11 x 13¹⁵⁄₁₆
(27.9 x 35.4)
Whitney Museum of American Art,
New York; Gift of Denise Rich
96.90.3

J. ALDEN WEIR
(1852–1919)

The Bridge: Nocturne (Nocturne:
Queensboro Bridge), c. 1910
Oil on canvas mounted on wood,
29 x 39½ (73.7 x 100.3)
Hirshhorn Museum and Sculpture
Garden, Smithsonian Institution,
Washington, D.C.; Gift
of Joseph H. Hirshhorn, 1966

The Plaza: Nocturne, 1911
Oil on canvas mounted on board,
29 x 39½ (73.7 x 100.3)
Hirshhorn Museum and Sculpture
Garden, Smithsonian Institution,
Washington, D.C.; Gift
of Joseph H. Hirshhorn, 1966

GUY C. WIGGINS
(1883–1962)

Metropolitan Tower, 1912
Oil on canvas, 34¹⁄₁₆ x 40⅛
(86.5 x 101.9)
The Metropolitan Museum of Art,
New York; George A. Hearn Fund,
1912

ANONYMOUS POLICE
PHOTOGRAPHY

Homicide Parlor/female victim in chair,
c. 1914–18 (1996 print)
Gelatin silver print, 8 x 10
(20.3 x 25.4)
New York City Police Department
Glass-Plate Negative Collection,
Municipal Archives, Department of
Records and Information Services,
City of New York

Homicide Pool Hall, c. 1914–18
(1996 print)
Gelatin silver print, 8 x 10
(20.3 x 25.4)
New York City Police Department
Glass-Plate Negative Collection,
Municipal Archives, Department of
Records and Information Services,
City of New York

Homicide victim wht male street view,
c. 1914–18 (1996 print)
Gelatin silver print, 8 x 10
(20.3 x 25.4)
New York City Police Department
Glass-Plate Negative Collection,
Municipal Archives, Department of
Records and Information Services,
City of New York

Murder Victim 1930S undersize (male),
c. 1914–18 (1996 print)
Gelatin silver print, 8 x 10
(20.3 x 25.4)
New York City Police Department
Glass-Plate Negative Collection,
Municipal Archives, Department of
Records and Information Services,
City of New York

UNKNOWN PHOTOGRAPHER

Partially Clad Skeleton of the
Flatiron Building, As Seen from Madison
Square, 1902
Gelatin silver print, mounted on
board, 9¹⁄₁₆ x 7¹⁄₁₆ (23.3 x 18.1)
Centre Canadien d'Architecture/
Canadian Centre for Architecture,
Montreal

Architectural Models

OWEN H. RAMSBURG

Model of Rockefeller Center,
early 1930s
Wood, 85½ x 51 x 55
Collection of The Rockefeller
Group, New York

Model of the Empire State Building, n.d.
Carved plaster, 80 x 29½ x 15¼
Museum of the City of New York

Fashion

LILLY DACHÉ
(1893–1990)

Hat, c. 1938
Wool half turban with velvet bow
Collection of Sandy Schreier

Hat, c. 1938
Ribbed velvet toque with bow
Collection of Sandy Schreier

JOHN FREDERICS
(1902–1993)

Hat, c. 1940
Wool felt with velvet crown,
band, and bow
Collection of Sandy Schreier

CHARLES JAMES
(1906–1978)

Hat, c. 1938
Plush hat with satin streamers
Collection of Sandy Schreier

Evening Bolero, 1954
Peau de soie with silk taffeta lining
Collection of Sandy Schreier

CLAIRE MCCARDELL
(1906–1958)

Gown, c. 1950
Striped dinner dress, cotton
and silk blend
Collection of Sandy Schreier

NORMAN NORELL
(1900–1972)

Hat, c. 1958
Velvet hat with bow
Collection of Sandy Schreier

VALENTINA
(1904–1989)

Hat, c. 1950
Plush cap with passementerie
and beads
Collection of Sandy Schreier

WOODMERE NEW YORK

Hat, c. 1935
Velvet with rhinestones, crystals,
and egret plume
Collection of Sandy Schreier

UNKNOWN DESIGNERS

Beaded dress, c. 1925
Beaded cotton with sequins,
beads, and pearls
Collection of Sandy Schreier

Beaded dress, c. 1925
Sequins on tulle with beaded fringe
Collection of Sandy Schreier

Hat, c. 1925
Cloche with jet beads and
beaded tassel
Collection of Sandy Schreier

Headdress, c. 1925
Beads, jet, and bakelite stars
Collection of Sandy Schreier

Films

Coney Island at Night, 1900–14.
Edison Company. 35mm film,
black-and-white, silent; 4 minutes.

**Interior, New York Subway, 14th Street to
42nd Street,** 1905. Biograph
Company. 35mm film, black-and-
white, silent; 4 minutes.

The Skyscrapers, 1907. Biograph
Company. 35mm film, black-
and-white, silent; 4 minutes.

The Musketeers of Pig Alley, 1912.
D.W. Griffith. 35mm film, black-
and-white, silent; 15 minutes.

Manhatta, 1921. Paul Strand and
Charles Sheeler. 35mm film, black-
and-white, silent; 9 minutes.

The City, 1939. Ralph Steiner
and Willard Van Dyke. 35mm film,
black-and-white, sound;
43 minutes.

In the Street, 1952. Helen Levitt,
Janice Loeb, James Agee. 16mm
film, black-and white, silent
with sound-on-cassette; 16 minutes.

Weegee's New York, 1953. Weegee
(Arthur Fellig). 16mm film, color,
sound; 20 minutes.

The Wonder Ring, 1955. Stan Brakhage.
16mm film, color, silent; 4 minutes.

Bridges-go-Round, 1958. Shirley
Clarke. 16mm film, color, sound;
4-minute film loop.

Broadway by Light, 1958. William
Klein. 35mm film, color, sound,
11 minutes.

Illustrated Works Not In the Exhibition

MAURICE PRENDERGAST
(1858–1924)

Sailboat Pond, Central Park, c. 1902
Watercolor on paper, 19¼ x 22³⁄₁₆
(48.9 x 56.4)
Whitney Museum of American Art,
New York; 50th Anniversary Gift of
an anonymous donor 86.57

JOHN SLOAN
(1871–1951)

Backyards, Greenwich Village, 1914
Oil on canvas, 26 x 32 (66 x 81.3),
Whitney Museum of American Art,
New York; Purchase 36.153

Assembling an exhibition on such a vast subject as New York is a daunting enterprise. I am indebted to David A. Ross, director, and Willard Holmes, deputy director, who inspired and supported the conception and execution of this exhibition. John G. Hanhardt stood by the project from the beginning, shaping its film component and advising on its design and conceptual structure. Claire Gilman and Corey Keller rallied to the excitement of the subject and did the amazing research that made this project possible. Corey Keller also attended to the many practical jobs involved with loan requests and the production of the catalogue, and in many cases made curatorial decisions about works to be included. We were all helped by Cassi Albinson, who joined the team and provided critical support in preparing both the exhibition and catalogue.

ACKNOWLEDGMENTS

Sandy Schreier advised in the choice of New York fashion for the exhibition. She generously lent garments from her collection and collaborated on their presentation. Cindy Sirko assisted with the execution of the costume display. Special thanks to Jon Gartenberg, who was curatorial adviser on the film section of the exhibition. His advice on all aspects of the film selection and preparation of the program was invaluable.

We owe a special debt to Brendan Gill—the dean of New York writers and long-time friend of the Whitney Museum—who generously graced this catalogue with his thoughts about artists and New York and, in the course of things, made some sly suggestions for a few works to be included in the show.

Among other colleagues who have made significant contributions, I would especially like to thank Tibor Kalman, who modestly calls himself exhibition designer, but who offered extraordinary insights and suggestions in the conceptualization of the project. Lana Hum, as architect of the installation, responded to Kalman's instincts about display and resourcefully provided solutions. Matthew Yokobosky, assistant curator, film and video, advised on the installation of film. Mary DelMonico inspired this book and she and the publications department nurtured it into existence. Barbara Glauber, assisted by Beverly Joel, conveyed her own sense of New York in the extraordinary design of this book. Constance Wolf, associate director for public programs, enthusiastically created public programming that will enhance the exhibition. Dan Okrent chose the literary texts used as exhibition labels.

I am extremely grateful to the many lenders who have made this exhibition possible. Although the Whitney Museum's collection is rich in New York art, we could not do a complete show based only on our holdings. Many museums and private collectors not only agreed to lend to the show, but also offered us a great deal of advice as we were assembling the exhibition. Their names are listed in the checklist at the end of this book. In particular, I would like to thank: Leslie Nolan, Museum of the City of New York; Sarah Greenough, National Gallery of Art, Washington, D.C.; Louise Désy and Nicholas Olsberg, Canadian Centre for Architecture, Montreal; Diana Edkins, Condé Nast Publications, Inc.; Howard Greenberg and Carrie Springer of the Howard Greenberg Gallery, New York; and Janet Lehr, Janet Lehr, Inc., New York. Finally, many individuals generously offered advice in areas in which they had particular expertise: Joanne Leonhardt Cassullo, Nigel Coates, Michelle Oka Donner, Mickey Friedman, Judith Gutman, Barbara Haskell, Steven Heller, Gary Hood, Wendy Kaplan, David Kiehl, Michelle McNally, Bibi Obler, Andrew Onraët, Luc Sante, and Robert Sklar.

E.S.

144